God Bless America: The Rosary

A Tool for Catholics and Protestants to Unite and Pray for the Healing of America

Stuart Walker

©2013 Stuart Walker. All rights reserved.

ISBN: 978-0-9893927-2-3

Cover Images:

Stars and Stripes of the American Flag ©iStockphoto.com/neustockimages
Rosary ©iStockphoto.com/mludzen

Rosary Image (pg 26):
©Marian Fathers of the Immaculate Conception of the B.V.M., used with permission

Scripture texts in this work are taken from the New American Bible with revised New Testament and Psalms © 1991, 1986, 1970 Confraternity of Christian Doctrine, Washington, D.C. and are used by permission of the copyright owner. All Rights Reserved. No part of the New American Bible may be reproduced in any form without permission in writing from the copyright owner

Library of Congress Control Number: 2013909761

Published by Walker Ministries, LLC
www.stuwalker.biz

A portion of the proceeds from sales of this book will go to the Christian Stewardship Foundation.

This book is dedicated to a young woman who at age 14 or 15 years old, had the courage, fortitude, and love strong enough to say "yes" to her God.

*That changed the world for all Eternity.
Once again, we ask her to come with us to intercede for America with its many wonders and its many flaws. We humble ourselves, as she did at the Wedding of Cana, when she intervened for the people who were out of wine.*

Father, we thank you for hearing our prayer. We, too, say "yes" for your will for America. Mary truly is "Blessed among women..." because of what you have done for her.

It is at her request that I have written this book to ask her intercession for America. I feel some positive changes coming soon.

Statement of Gratitude

I would also like to express my gratitude to God and to Mary for bringing a young woman into my life to assist me in the publishing of this book, Patti Frazee. Patti is not Catholic, and it is this giftedness and openmindedness that brought much insight to my message. It was Patti, for example, who reminded me that Protestants did not know how to pray the Rosary and that I should include some form of instruction in how to do so. Hence, we have the *How to Use This Book* section (which Patti wrote for me) and several [ ] bracketed sections. It was in those areas where she felt more information would be helpful to assist someone who had not prayed a Rosary before.

I am very grateful for her insight. God always seems to provide the right people at the right time.

Table of Contents

Preface vii
Introduction...1
How to Develop a "Prayer Strategy"...............15
How to Use This Book.....................................23
The Prayers that Make Up the Rosary 25
The "Mysteries" of the Rosary 31
Let the Intercession Begin...............................37
Prayers for Those Who Govern 41

Preface

I believe every generation has said to itself, "What is going on? Things are deteriorating so badly. I feel like this country is falling apart at the seams."

There are many reasons to feel hopeful in our country today, but one cannot whitewash the facts either. We are more corrupt in our country, in politics, yes, sadly, and even in our Churches; Catholic and Protestant. But there is always hope. We have the choice of turning to ask God's grace.

My wife Cathy and I have read a book *To the Priests, Our Lady's Beloved Sons*, by The Marian Movement of Priests. It is a beautiful book, full of hope and promise. However, it is also unvarnished Truth as Mary shares with her beloved priests the pain on her heart and the heart of her beloved Son, Jesus Christ.

There are two stages of a theme listed in this book: personal repentance and the powerful promises of what our world *could be like* if we but turn our hearts back toward God.

First — **personal repentance.** The book is written for priests so it is addressed in the masculine gender. Please just substitute "man/woman", for the truths belong to both genders. The following are selections from the book, printed with permission.

The New Man Within #401

COME HOLY SPIRIT, COME BY MEANS OF THE POWERFUL INTERCESSION OF THE IMMACULATE HEART OF MARY, YOUR WELL-BELOVED SPOUSE.

Mary, I place myself in the cradle of your Immaculate Heart.

Let there die in you today all that you have inherited from the first man. And let there emerge at last into the light the new man, who is born in the new sepulcher where Christ is risen in the glorious splendor of his divinity:

The new man of grace and holiness,
The new man of love and communion,
The new man of mercy and purity,
The new man of humility and charity,
The new man of docility and of obedience,
The new man of light and sanctity,
The new man of form in the new sepulcher and who come to life at the joyous moment of the resurrection of Christ.

I am forming you in your hearts, in order to bring you to conversion and to open you to a new capacity for love. In this way, I heal you of the malady of egoism and of aridity.

I am forming you in your souls, helping you to cultivate in them the great gift of divine grace, of purity and of charity. And, as in a heavenly garden, I am bringing to blossom the flowers of all the virtues which cause you to grow in holiness. Thus, I remove from you the shadow of evil, the coldness of sin, the wilderness of impurity.

I am forming you in your bodies, causing to shine forth in them the light of the Spirit who is dwelling there as in a living temple of his. Thus I lead you along the way of purity, of beauty, of harmony, of joy, of peace, of communion with all paradise.

I urge you to consecrate yourselves to my Immaculate Heart, entrusting yourself to me as little children, so that I may be able to lead you along the road of holiness, in the joyous practice of all the virtues: of faith, of hope, of charity, of prudence, of fortitude, of justice, of temperance, of silence, of humility, of purity, of mercy.

—From *To the Priests, Our Lady's Beloved Sons*, The Marian Movement of Priests

Here the hand that rocked the cradle in which Jesus lay, and formed His youth, forms—through prayer—Our Hearts and lives as we yield to her love.

He will use you to accomplish great things, on the condition that you believe much more in His love than in your own weakness.
—Mother Teresa

I am deeply touched by the Mother of Our Lord Jesus Christ's invitation to allow her to pray with me to her Son and our Redeemer. Since I have begun obeying this request, I have seen a tremendous growth in my spiritual and prayer life. I guess I would call it a "spiritual spurt" of growth. Sins I have been struggling with for years have dissipated to the point where they are basically nonexistent.

My relationship with Christ has become much more intimate and the desire to serve Him even stronger than before. I meditate on these words often.

As I have prayed the prayer we in the Catholic Church call the *Magnificat*, I meditate upon the fact of Mary's intercession with faith, just as I would feel comforted by the prayers of my friends and family in time of need.

> My soul magnifies the Lord
> And my spirit rejoices in God my Savior;
> Because He has regarded the lowliness of his handmaid;
> For behold, henceforth all generations shall call me blessed;
> Because he who is mighty has done great things for me, and holy is his name;
> And his mercy is from generation to generation
> on those who fear him.
> He has shown might with his arm,
> He has scattered the proud in the conceit of their heart.
> He has put down the mighty from their thrones,
> and has exalted the lowly.
> He has filled the hungry with good things,
> and the rich he has sent away empty.
> He has given help to Israel, his servant, mindful of his mercy
> Even as he spoke to our fathers, to Abraham and to his posterity forever.   *Luke 1:46-55*

The word *Magnificat* comes from the Latin, "to magnify." It has been referred to as "Mary's Song," or Mary's praise of God for her child bearing. It is common Judeo/Christian heritage to celebrate victories when God brings them to pass in a person's life.

It is a good spiritual exercise to meditate upon and think about these words and observe how God has worked in your life! Notice how all the good and wonderful things that have happened in Mary's life are attributed to God, not Mary herself—a good example for us. She takes no credit for anything in her life other than to say "yes" to God's will for her life — a humble characteristic to be emulated.

Mary, like Christ, prays constantly for the Church and for you and me. In John 19:27, in his dying last words, Jesus presents Mary to John as the mother of the Church.

Cardinal Jorge Mario Bergoglio of Argentina was elected Pope Francis and has been chosen as the successor to Pope Benedict XVI. With him are also a number of "new" beginnings for the Church.

He is the first Pope in history to be chosen from the Americas (North, Central, and South America); he is the first Pope to choose the name Francis. This name represents two wonderful Saints of the Catholic Church. St. Francis of Assisi, who renounced a wealthy dissolute lifestyle in 1209 and embraced, rather, a lifestyle of poverty (spiritual and physical) and simplicity. He was instructed by God to "Rebuild My Church." Today, once again, God's church, as well as God's world, is broken and needs to be restructured. The other saint was St. Francis Xavier, founder of the Jesuit Order of Priests. He was known as the "Evangelist's Pope" for his work in spreading the Gospel to parts of the world that had never heard the Good News of Jesus Christ.

In Jesuit spirituality, Ignatius of Loyola, one of the most prominent teachers of Jesuit spirituality, often used meditation and imagination in the quest to come closer to God. In one of his exercises, he talks of the "Triple Colloquy" (conversation, dialogue, conference). He suggests this meditation that I have enhanced for this occasion:

One, imagine you are in a conversation with Mary, the Mother of Christ, the Son of God. At the wedding of Cana, Mary went to Jesus with a simple piece of information: "They are out of wine." She gave no instructions to Jesus about how to solve the problems, she just presented her Son with the need that was present.

In our scenario, we do not tell God how to fix the United States, we simply approach Mary and tell her, "Mary, the United States has left the Godly principles it was founded upon." We then visualize and ask Mary to accompany us as we approach Jesus. One can only imagine how powerful this prayer, or conversation, with Mary and Jesus could be. Jesus, as at Cana, will instruct those necessary to carry out His wishes, reminiscent of the Wine Steward.

The next scene, you and Mary are together in the presence of Jesus, the Savior of the world. Again, the prayer is simply, "Jesus, the United States has left the Godly principles it was founded upon. It needs a Redeemer."

The next scene visualizes you, Mary, and Jesus, appearing before the Throne of God. There, the following conversation takes place. Jesus says, "Father, I thank you for hearing our prayers. It is reported to me that the United States of America has sadly left the beautiful principles and Godly love upon which this great country was founded. They need redemption. Father, I respectfully remind you that I have died on the Cross, according to your Will for the sins of these people as well as the sins of the World. I ask you to, in My name, honor the request of these people, presented by My Mother, Mary, and send the Holy Spirit to renew the hearts of those who will listen to your Word and turn back to your Love for them. I have forgiven them, and you have forgiven them, because you and I are One. Send a new Pentecost, a new Revival through Our Holy Spirit to bring them back to us."

It is with this Faith we look at what the possibility could be for the United States. It would be breathtaking.

The second promise from *To the Priests, Our Lady's Beloved Sons* is for renewal of our society and **what our country could be like.**

The Holy Spirit Will Come #383

The Holy Spirit will come, as heavenly dew of grace and of fire, which will renew all the world. Under His irresistible action of love, the Church will open itself to live the new era of its greatest holiness and will shine resplendently with so strong a light that it will attract to itself all the nations of the earth.

The Holy Spirit will come, that the Will of the Heavenly Father be accomplished and the created universe once again reflect his great glory.

The Holy Spirit will come, to establish the glorious reign of Christ, and it will be a reign of grace, of holiness, of love, of justice and of peace. With his divine love, He will open the doors of hearts and illuminate all consciences. Every person will see himself in the burning fire of divine truth. It will be like a judgment in miniature. And then Jesus Christ will bring his glorious reign in the world.

The Holy Spirit will come, by means of triumph of my Immaculate Heart. For this, I am calling upon you all today to enter into the cenacle of my Heart. Thus you will be prepared to receive the gift of the Holy Spirit which will transform you and make you the instruments of which Jesus will establish his reign.

—From *To the Priests, Our Lady's Beloved Sons*,
The Marian Movement of Priests

In Scripture, it tells us that the job of the Holy Spirit is to a) convict us of our sinfulness, b) of the righteousness of Jesus, and c) that the things of this world have passed away. The sin of materialism is rampant in our world. Not just consumer goods, but the trust we should be putting in God is transferred to the material realm; things we can see, smell, taste, and touch. Our country suffers from deep "spiritual needs."

The name Holy Spirit is, in itself, a descriptive term. There are many "spirits" in the world. We give head knowledge to the term "evil" spirits, liquor stores sell Wine and "Spirits." That term signifies that in their world, literally, the *life* has been distilled out of the grains that make up the beverage and all that remains is the "spirit" of the grains. So, "Holy" (set apart from the spirits of this world) signifies that the Holy Spirit is set apart to help us live our lives according to the righteousness of God. Without God's presence in our lives that would not be possible.

Come Lord Jesus #397

Come, Lord Jesus, in the life of each one, by means of Divine Grace, of love and of sanctity. I will act in a very powerful way to bring you, who have consecrated yourselves to my Immaculate Heart, to a great sanctity, so that Jesus may live, work and shine forth more and more in your life.

Come, Lord Jesus, in families, to help them to rediscover the life of communion, of mutual and reciprocal love, of perfect unity and of complete availability to the gift of life.

Come, Lord Jesus, in nations, which have need of becoming once again communities open to the spiritual and material needs of all, especially of the little, the needy, the sick, the poor and the marginalized.

> —From *To the Priests, Our Lady's Beloved Sons,*
> The Marian Movement of Priests

The name Jesus means "Savior." What I wish to accomplish with this book is to have every Christian, regardless of which Denomination one embraces, preemptively acknowledge what the world for all Eternity will acknowledge whether they confess it now or not:

> *Have among yourselves the same attitude that is also yours in Christ Jesus, Who, though he was in the form of God, did not regard equality with God something to be grasped. Rather, he emptied himself, taking the form of a slave, coming in human likeness; and found human in appearance, he humbled himself, becoming obedient to death, even death on a cross.*
>
> **Because of this, God greatly exalted him and bestowed on him the name that is above every name, that at the name of Jesus every knee should bend, of those in heaven and on earth and under the earth, and every tongue confess that Jesus Christ is Lord, to the glory of God the Father.** (Philippians 2:5-11)

May the Blood that flowed from your sacred wounds soften the hardness of my heart and bring me to true charity.

—Rachelle Linner
Give Us This Day, June 2012, pg. 5

Introduction

He drew a circle that shut me out—
Heretic, rebel, a thing to flout.
But love and I had the wit to win:
We drew a circle and took him In!
—**Edwin Markham**

I grew up in the Catholic faith and struggled with one important issue my whole life: People who were Catholic versus people who were "Protestant." I always felt there was an "us versus them" mentality. It caused a lot of tension within me. Why? Because I had been raised to believe that *only Catholics* were going to Heaven. Yet, my mother was Catholic; my father was not. My maternal grandfather was Catholic, but my maternal grandmother was not. My only brother married a woman who was not Catholic.

When I met and married a Lutheran woman, I discovered that she felt no concern about not being Catholic. The reason? She had been brought up Lutheran and was told that *only Lutherans* were going to Heaven!

How we, as humans, have complicated Gods plan of salvation. Jesus simply asked for two or three to agree in His Name. Think of the Power of God's Grace if thousands asked God to send Redeeming Grace upon His people.

This booklet is for all my Catholic brothers and sisters, and an outreach to my Protestant brothers and sisters, to unite in a common strategy to pray to God for the conversion of the United States of America. In my mind, it is not "what" you believe in, it is "who" you believe in. There is no doubt in my mind that all Christians pray for our leaders, as Scriptures encourage us to do. Think of the possibilities of thousands of Christians coming together, united in one voice, repenting of our divisions, and seeking God's mercy on America.

We all feel a sense of urgency with the direction our beloved country is going. The United States is under a Spiritual threat, the likes of which we have never witnessed before. The coin of our realm, the inscriptions on our Federal buildings and in our Courtrooms, all speak to this Truth: *"In God We Trust."* The question that comes to my mind is, "If we all trust in God, why are we so divided?" It is perplexing.

We can easily learn from the sports world of what could happen in the Kingdom of God if we were united. Anyone with the slightest interest in sports knows that "chemistry," or team unity, is what wins championships. Players unite under one coach. They listen, they apply the instructions to their particular position in the interest of team unity, and they teach those same instructions to players who are their understudies. In other words, they put aside personal interests for the benefit of the team. Why can't we, as Christians, do the same?

We know that all Christians subscribe to the belief that there is one Sovereign God who is the Creator of the world, who is Father to all who will believe in Him. He is a God of love, who brings love, mercy, and forgiveness to those who call on His name.

We, as Christians, are united in our belief that Jesus is the Messiah (John 4:25, 26) whose name is Emmanuel (*God with us*). We believe, as the Son of God and the Son of Man, that He was crucified, died, and was buried. We believe that the Power of God conquered death and raised Him from the dead and that He will come to judge the living and the dead. That is the common Creed we adhere to as our statement of Faith.

We know, as Christians, it is the will of God that all people experience Salvation to spend Eternity with Him. Paul tells the Romans, "For those he foreknew he also predestined to be conformed to the image of his Son, so that he might be the firstborn among many brothers. And those he predestined he also called; and those he called he also justified; and those he justified he also glorified." (Romans 8:29-30)

Sadly, within that statement is also reality. "For those he foreknew he also predestined to be conformed to the image of his Son..." Not all people will heed the call of God to come to Him. God gives people free will to accept Him or reject Him. However, many of those who have chosen Him get sidetracked by the seduction of the worldly ways. It is for those we pray to call back into His Will.

We believe, commonly, that God sent His promised Holy Spirit to breathe life and strength to complete His mission to bring the Good News of Salvation and Baptism of all...in the name of the Father, the Son, and the Holy Spirit. (Matthew 28:19-20)

We believe there are evil spirits in the world, the leader of whom is satan. His express purpose is to thwart that very mission in whatever way he can. His one desire is to cause Spiritual death to those God has created to spend eternity with Him.

So our hope is to find a tool that we can accept, based upon Scripture, to fight the Spiritual Warfare needed to allow the Holy

Spirit to free the captives who have fallen under the spell of the worldly teachings and philosophies. Over the years, these man-made philosophies have failed to work.

A Spiritual Tool

In the Gospel, Jesus teaches us, *"If a kingdom is divided against itself, that kingdom cannot stand. And if a house is divided against itself, that house will not be able to stand..."* (Mark 3:24-25) This was a conversation in regard to the fact that some of the Jews, while Jesus was teaching in the Synagogue, accused him: "The scribes who had come from Jerusalem said, *'He is possessed by Beelzebub,'* and *'By the prince of demons he drives out demons.'"* (Mark 3:22)

Man *alone* cannot and will not heal the divisions that exist in our society today, but traditionally, those who adhere to the Judeo/Christian principles of love, the respect of each person, and presence of God in our midst, can serve God by calling on His name for guidance, mercy, and restoration.

Imagine the power if we, as brothers and sisters in Christ, can find a tool that both small "c" and large "C" Christians can use as a prayer strategy to come together as a family. The small "c" means universal Christianity. The large "C" refers to the denomination of Catholicism. Together, we can petition God to bring unity those who have accepted Jesus as their personal Savior, and are attempting to turn their lives over to him and live under his Lordship. When we focus on "Who" we believe in, we create unity; when we focus on "what" we believe in, we breed division and misfortune because satan accomplishes *his* mission of *divide and conquer.* Jesus is not *glorified*; he continues to be *crucified.*

I would like to tell you of a "secret" weapon, a weapon so powerful that it can change the course of nations without firing a single shot. A weapon so potent it can change the hearts of enemies that are filled with nothing but hatred to hearts that are filled with love. A weapon so prevailing that the hardest heart will be melted under the fullnes of its love.

This "secret" weapon is really no secret at all; at least to Catholics. It is called the Rosary. The Rosary has been a weapon employed by Catholics for years against "Spiritual Enemies."

In the interest of full disclosure, let me say that my interest in this has peaked over the past three to five years because of my personal experience with this area of spirituality. When I was a child, I was taught the Rosary and told to recite it frequently. It was boring. I ended up feeling guilty because my mind wandered, I fell asleep, and it just did not register very deeply with my spirit. Then, something happened that changed the way I thought about the Rosary.

I was in Wisconsin giving a talk at a Catholic Church. I had visited with the priest about the struggles I was having with this form of spirituality. The priest happened to have a deep devotion to Mary and the Rosary.

The Church building was back-to-back to the rectory where the priest lived and, during the Offertory of the Mass, the priest left the altar. I thought he needed an emergency visit to the restroom and thought nothing more of it. However, he didn't return for a long time and I began to get concerned. Finally, after the collection had been taken and we were close to the part of the Mass that involved the Consecration of the host and wine, he did return. I breathed a sigh of relief.

Suddenly, he walked to the front of the altar and said, "I am going to ask Mr. Walker to step forward, please." I reluctantly did so.

In his hands was a beautiful green-beaded Rosary. He said,

"This is one of my favorite Rosaries. The inscription is written in Gaelic. If you can translate it, I will give you the Rosary."

I gratefully said, "You get to keep the Rosary, Father; I don't speak Gaelic."

"I figured as much. I want to give you this in thanksgiving for your talk this morning." He handed me the Rosary and I walked back to my seat.

As Mass continued, I said a prayer. "Lord, the Mass is the most important celebration of our Catholic faith. It is not to be interrupted by or for anything. It is our worship of you. If you have put it on the heart of this priest to stop the Mass to get this Rosary and present it to me in front of everyone, I must take a second look at my attitude toward this prayer style. Please open my eyes and my heart."

Then, the Lord began to work in my spirit about some of my attitudes toward the recitation of the Rosary. One of the insights was that the "mysteries," as they are called, are actually meditations on various events in the life of the Holy Family: Joseph, Mary, and Jesus.

This is not intended to be a theological discussion on the Rosary, just some thoughts I have worked with. It has brought me great comfort and peace of mind. I feel led to share this with my non-Catholic brothers and sisters, only because I wish you the Joy I have experienced on my journey.

The Power of the Rosary

One issue that seems very divisive between Catholics and Protestants is role of Mary in Salvation. She is prophesied throughout the Old Testament, just as is the promised Messiah. ***"Therefore the Lord himself [God] shall give you a sign; Behold, a virgin shall conceive, and bear a son and shall call his name Immanuel."*** (Isaiah 7:14) **In the New Testament, we**

see the fulfillment of the Prophesy of Isaiah. The angel Gabriel appears to a "Virgin" named Mary. (Luke 3:26-33)

I wonder if we all believe the same Truth but we are expressing it in different ways. Are we not doing what Paul talks about in his first letter to the Corinthians? Simply:

Brothers & sisters, I could not talk to you as spiritual people, but as fleshly people, as infants in Christ. I fed you milk, not solid food, because you were unable to take it. Indeed, you are still not able, even now, for you are still of the flesh. While there is jealousy and rivalry among you, are you not of the flesh, and behaving in an ordinary human way?

Whenever someone says, "I belong to Paul," and another, "I belong to Apollos," are you not merely human? What is Apollos, after all, and what is Paul? Ministers through whom you became believers, just as the Lord assigned each one.

I planted, Apollos watered, but God caused the growth. Therefore, neither the one who plants nor the one who waters is anything, but only God, who causes the growth. The one who plants and the one who waters are equal, and each will receive wages in proportion to his labor. For we are God's co-workers; you are God's field, God's building. (I Corinthians 3:1-9)

Just as Paul asked the Corinthians to set aside their differences and focus on Jesus as the head of the Church, I am asking for all Christians to put aside differences and unify under the banner of love for God and honoring Mary's request to pray for the United States of America.

I am calling for the Catholics and Protestants to come

together and join in petitioning Mary to go to her Son to deliver this beautiful nation from the evil that has come over it.

I have found that my Protestant friends resist the title *Mary, Mother of God*. They tend to see that statement as proclaiming Mary as being greater than God. They are correct in rejecting *that* idea. That is not what the Catholic Church teaches and Mary herself would reject that idea completely. The Gospel does, however, teach that Mary was chosen "among women" for the task of providing the birthing process for Jesus. She was told that His name was to be called Jesus (Savior) and Emmanuel (God with us). In the sense that Jesus is God/man and cannot be separated, Mary is the Mother of God.

As Christians, we understand that our "warfare" is not conventional. That is, we do not fight against each other but our battles are in the heavenly realm. So we use spiritual weapons or prayers.

One of the Truths that separate true Christians from false Christians is whether they receive Jesus with the true nature of God and the true nature of man. To reject either notion is to reject the sovereignty of God to do what He wants to do. If Mary is the mother of Jesus, then she is also the Mother of God. The Church teaches that one cannot separate the two.

I would like to introduce you to a style of prayer we, as Catholics, have used for hundreds of years to ask the Blessed Virgin Mary, the mother of Christ, to intercede on behalf of the citizens of the United States of America.

It is told that during the Battle of New Orleans, the British were winning the battle and the Catholics prayed the Rosary, asking Mary to intercede on their behalf. As they prayed, the tide of the battle turned and the Battle of New Orleans was won against the British. Several countries around the world can testify to similar events.

Mexicans tell the story of Our Lady of Guadalupe where

Mary was prominent in Church history. In 1583, Mary appeared to a peasant named Juan Diego. She told him she wanted him to go to the Bishop and ask him to pray to her, asking for her help. At first, the Bishop was not interested, but through a sign one would call a miracle, he consented and she became the patron saint of Mexico.

In the world we live in today, one does not experience much love. In the news media, we are in a time where criticism is the preferred form of communication. We spend a lot of negative energy fighting over issues. The Catholic-based inspirational organization *The Christopher's* (www.christophers.org) has offered the slogan, "It is better to light one little candle than to curse the darkness."

For years, the Blessed Virgin Mary asked that the Pope consecrate Russia to her beloved heart so she could call on her Son to take action. Finally, the hierarchy complied, and when they did, the USSR dissolved peacefully, without firing a shot.

So why don't we take comfort from these historical events and learn our lesson. Come together and pray the Rosary, asking God to convert America—not to turn *to* Catholicism, but to turn from our unrighteous ways, secularism, and repent—to turn from our present sinfulness and obey Godly precepts (read Psalm 119).

Secularism Humanism trusts in the individual to resolve their problems and in the Government to provide not only for their needs, but for all the hedonistic desires as well. This "religion" focuses on dependency on Government and is diametrically opposed to the founding father's proclamation, "In God We Trust." That was recognition of the Judeo/Christian creed accepted by our founding fathers even though not all were Christian or Jewish.

The Kingdom of God is not taken by violence, but by peace. Jesus is the Prince of Peace.

The History of the Rosary

The Rosary came to pass so ordinary people could approach God and learn the events of the Life of Christ. The Monks were educated and could read. The people could not. So the Monks taught them a "bouquet" (50) prayers focusing on the events in the Life of Christ. When they left the Monastery, they would recite this bouquet, saying one Our Father (the prayer Jesus taught the Apostles to pray) as a sign of unity with each other and with Jesus (Our Father). They then followed this with five sets of 10 Hail Mary's following the Our Father. In this way, the illiterate people could follow the life of Christ, calling on Mary to give insight into those events.

The Rosary format was given to St. Dominic by Mary in 1214 AD. St. Dominic saw how grave the sins of the people of his time were and how these sins were hindering their conversion and their relationship with God.

He was told by Mary that there were the same number of Hail Mary's in the Rosary as there were Psalms (150) in the Scripture. However, the people were illiterate and could not read the Psalms. By praying the Rosary they could grow in faith by focusing on the events in the life of Christ.

The Rosary was created of three parts, called mysteries, with five decades each (this will be explained later).

This was a way for the poor people to meditate on the Life (Joyful Mysteries), death (Sorrowful Mysteries), and the Glory of Jesus and His Resurrection, the honor of His mother Mary, and the virtues they practiced (Glorious Mysteries). The Rosary beads were meant simply to keep track to where they were in the process, a practice that is found in several religions including the Jewish tradition of prayer beads. Pope John Paul II in 2002 added a fourth Decade called the Luminous Mysteries or "Mysteries of Light," focusing on the events in Christ's public ministry.

For many, praying the Rosary meets the command to

"...pray without ceasing..." (1 Thessalonians 5:17), especially in times of trial when other prayers or words may not flow freely. Many feel inadequate in their prayer life before God, and the Rosary is a simple tool to keep them focused on His Goodness.

Our Commonality as Christians

I started praying the Rosary more diligently after a trip to Florida and an encounter with the Patriotic Rosary. I found that, as I prayed for our nation's leaders, both on the Federal and State level, I found a deeper sense of peace. I had been doing this already through another prayer of intercession, but this seemed to articulate what I wanted to say through my recitation of the Rosary. Even more thrilling than that, I found myself relaxing and I truly felt a sense of God's presence in my life and his mercy and forgiveness flowing *through* me to the people I was praying for. The anger I had was gone; replaced by serenity. The fear I had was now gone; replaced by Joy. While we were in Florida, Mary spoke to me and said, "I want you to take the Rosary to the Protestants. I will honor their prayers as well."

This booklet is dedicated to that thought. I want to build a bridge between my denomination, the "Catholic Church," and the "catholic Christians" around the world. After all, we serve the same God, we accept the same Personal Savior, and we understand that this country was founded on Judeo/Christian principles of belief in God, respect for human life and dignity, and each individual's right to worship the God of their understanding. Besides, isn't the idea of "one religion for all" exactly why we rebelled against the British? I truly believe that as we come together in this universal appeal to God to deliver this nation from the evil that has come upon us, God will honor our petition and heal our nation and "deliver us from Evil." That is not a call for One Religion; it is a call for unity among Christians for a common cause.

Let's look at some of the things I feel we have in common as Christians:

1. We accept the "mono-Theological" principle—One God.
2. We accept that God created the world from chaos into something beautiful and wonderful to share with us.
3. We accept that, in some way, evil came into this world that God created.

My vision is that people would come together from all denominations to embrace a prayer "*strategy*" to take back America from the darkness of the evil one that has come upon it. It is a strategy that has worked for centuries. I believe it is an accomplishable act if we focus on Christ, as Paul describes. Christ is not divided into denominations. Again, when we focus on *who* we believe in, we create unity. When we focus on *what* we believe in, we begin to cause division and satan wins.

There is one passage in Scripture that is the desire of my heart to see God bring to fruition. In John 17, Jesus pours out His heart to the Father, knowing He is going to the cross. It is sometimes referred to as the "High Priestly prayer" of Jesus. In that prayer, Jesus yearns of one thing for his disciples from His Father: *I pray for them. I do not pray for the world but for the ones you have given me, because they are yours, and everything of mine is yours and everything of yours is mine, and I have been glorified in them. And now I will no longer be in the world, but they are in the world, while I am coming to you. Holy Father, keep them in your name that you have given me,* ***so that they may be one just as we are.*** (John 17:9-11)

How painful it must be for Our Savior to see the divisions within those who call themselves by His name. Can we deny Jesus the one desire of His heart? Is Jesus, sitting on his throne at the right had of the Father, still praying that prayer? "So that *they* may be one *just as we are.*" That plea certainly makes me want to work for healing, not division.

We, as Christians, seem to have lost our direction, spiritually. People cling to their denominational beliefs because they are comfortable. Everyone seeks their own pathway to heaven. However, true spirituality does not seek to serve self, the Holy Spirit teaches us to seek to serve others. God is often presented as a mamby-pamby God who will accept anyone who has good thoughts and says nice things. Once in a while, we can even throw in random acts of kindness to make us feel good. There is nothing wrong with feeling good, however, we must ask what is our motivation? "Am I doing this to make me feel good; or is it doing the Will of My Father that makes me feel good?" If God does not call you to participate in this strategy of prayer, stop doing it, or at least until you find the "Peace that passes all understanding."

In these times, I feel sadness in my heart for those friends who miss the blessings of honoring the Mother of their Savior. When I was growing up I remember how much some of my friends' mothers influenced my life. I know how *my mother* influenced my life. As a Catholic, I see how my improved relationship with Mary has had an exceptional influence in my life and my relationship with Christ. As my relationship with Mary grows deeper through the Rosary, I now feel more like a "family" member. I hope, after reading some of the following explanations of the "spirituality" behind the Rosary, you — Catholic or Protestant — will consider joining those who are uniting in praying the Rosary for the healing of our country.

Stuart H. Walker
A Servant of Love

How to Develop a "Prayer Strategy"

We are in Spiritual Warfare. That terminology is used throughout the Scriptures, especially in the New Testament. The analogy is one people can relate to, although they know very little about war, except what they see on TV.

To win a war, one must have a "strategy." A strategy is simply a preparation of action premeditated to achieve a particular objective. For example, in 12-Step Spirituality, the Second Step states, "We came to believe that a power greater than our ability could restore us to sanity." The "strategy" is to acknowledge that we need help, that there is, in the universe, a power greater than human ability to accomplish the objective of living a sane or serene life. It is an accepted philosophy in the 12-Step programs and has been a source of healing for millions who were trapped in the slavery of different self-destructive influences. As Christians, our "Higher Power" is Jesus Christ. The word "Christian" means "follower of Christ." It was Jesus who said, "I am the Way, the Truth, and the Life." Early believers were called members of "The

Way." This described people who had chosen to believe that Jesus was, in fact, God's Son and, as such, was truly God, and truly man. *We* are truly human, we are not God, we are made only in the *image* of God. We contain godly nature, but it is broken in Spirit. The original sin of Adam and Eve was not eating from the forbidden fruit. The true original sin was the desire to be like God, or even greater than God.

For years I have admired the forcefulness of prayer my non-Catholic friends prayed when they prayed Scriptures, believing in the passage from Ephesians, *And take the helmet of salvation and the sword of the Spirit, which is the word of God.* (Ephesians 6:17) Their prayers seemed very powerful and they seemed just as confident in its ability to accomplish what they wanted. Suddenly, as I thought about the Rosary, it dawned on me that the prayers of the Rosary were all from Scripture (the Word of God) passages. And the highest power was that Jesus is the Word. That is how John introduces his Gospel. *In the beginning was the Word, and the Word was with God, and the Word was God.* (John 1:1)

For hundreds of years, Catholics have prayed a series of prayers that make up what is called "the Rosary." The name *rosary* comes from the flower, the rose, long a symbol of love. The rose has, in the Catholic Church, stood for Mary, the woman God chose as the birth-mother of His beloved Son, Jesus.

One of the first questions that arises with non-Catholics is, "Why pray to Mary. Why not pray directly to Jesus?"

This is a fair and reasonable question and it is also raised about praying *to* the saints. Catholics pray *through* the saints, as they pray *through* Mary, not *to* Mary. This is a misunderstood concept by many non-Catholics. On the other hand, those same Christians have no issue with going to a friend and saying, "Pray for me." Friends do not deify friends by asking them to pray for them, they are simply asking for help. Catholics do not Deify Mary by praying the Rosary, they are simply asking for her to help.

No, compassionately we join them in prayers of petition for Jesus to respond to their prayers in the same way the people in Jesus's time either carried their loved ones or brought them to Jesus. In either case, Jesus commended the efforts with healing either through the faith of the individual, or through the faith of those who brought them.

Some people have great faith—such as Peter who had no problem going directly to Jesus, even sometimes with misdirected thought pattern—and others feared Jesus because of his power. Fear has two sources: one is to cower before as in fear of being rebuked or destroyed, and the other one of being so in awe of the person they are restrained from approaching. God is to be held in reverence. However, because God is love and we rely on the finished work of Christ on the Cross, He is always approachable.

An objective description of the Rosary can be found on one of the present-day sources, Wikipedia:

> The **Rosary** (from Latin rosarium, meaning "rose garden") or "garland of roses" is a popular and traditional Catholic devotion. The term denotes the prayer beads used to count the series of prayers that make up the rosary. The prayers consist of repeated sequences of the Lord's Prayer followed by ten prayings of the Hail Mary and a single praying of "Glory Be to the Father" and is sometimes accompanied by the Fatima Prayer; each of these sequences is known as a decade. The praying of each decade is accompanied by meditation on one of the Mysteries of the Rosary, which recall the life of Jesus Christ.

The traditional 15 Mysteries of the Rosary were standardized, based on the long-standing custom, by Pope St. Pius V in the 16th century. The mysteries are grouped into three sets: the joyful mysteries, the sorrowful mysteries, and the glorious mysteries. In 2002, Pope John Paul II announced five new optional mysteries, the Luminous Mysteries, bringing the total number of mysteries to 20."

http://en.wikipedia.org/wiki/Rosary

From this we see that we, as Christians are called to the "rose garden," to pray. No, not literally, but it is a metaphor for finding a place of *solitude* to commune with God our Father. This was a common practice in the life of Jesus. Every Christian is taught that prayer is communion with God or discussion with God and is essential to attempting to live the life God wants us to live. However, without Power of the Holy Spirit, we cannot live the life God calls us to live in this world.

Jesus even thought the subject so important that when his disciples asked him how they should do it, he gave them specific instructions on how to pray. That alone is a beautiful study of the petitions we pray to our God for on a daily basis.

One aspect of prayer that is important is that it be biblical. As mentioned in the Wikipedia article, there are 20 so-called "mysteries" involved in the Rosary. Eighteen of these focus on an event in the Life of Christ, with two of them focusing on the rewards given to His mother. The word mystery is not that we cannot understand something, it is the fact that we trust God in our prayers to reveal his will and how and when he chooses to accomplish his will as we walk in our Faith journey.

In the Our Father, one of our petitions, "...lead us not into temptation, but deliver us from evil..." is the part we wish to focus upon. If there is any doubt in one's mind that there is evil in our land, one only has to pick up a daily newspaper, or turn on the TV. There is a lot of ugliness in the world, as there is a lot of love. I am convinced the number one illiness in the world today, and in our United States is the feeling of loneliness and abandonment.

So often when I hear a call for prayer for this country, it is a quote from 2 Chronicles when Solomon petitions God to help him lead God's people.

> *The Lord appeared to Solomon during the night and said to him: "I have heard your prayer, and I have chosen this place for my house of sacrifice.*
>
> *"If I close heaven so that there is no rain, if I command the locust to devour the land, if I send pestilence among my people, and <u>if my people, upon whom my name has been pronounced, humble themselves and pray, and seek my presence and turn from their evil ways, I will hear them from heaven and pardon their sins and revive their land.</u>*
>
> *"Now my eyes shall be open and my ears attentive to the prayer of this place. And now I have chosen and consecrated this house that my name may be there forever; my eyes and my heart also shall be there always."*
> 2 Chronicles 7:12-16 (emphasis added)

As we look closely at this, the Lord hears and answers Solomon. He confirms this with: "...I have heard your prayer, and I have chosen this place for my house of sacrifice." God chose it, not Solomon. God is the Creator and has the right to choose what or whomever he desires to do his will.

In reading the passage carefully, we see a covenant between God and Solomon, however, that covenant calls for repentance on the part of the people.

God' Part

God listened to Solomon and God chose the temple as *His* house of Sacrifice.

God has the right and the ability to close up heaven or open heaven to his people. God has the capability to command locusts to devour the land as He did in Egypt. He can send pestilence among His people. God created everything, seen and unseen, and God can and will cause calamity to get the attention of His people who are in disobedience. Not as punishment, but chastisement with the intent to have them turn back to Him. Any good, loving parent will chastise their child when they misbehave or become defiant.

Our Part

"If my people, who are called by my name..." In those days, the Jews were called by His name, His chosen ones. Today, both the Jews and Christians are "...those called by his name..." As His people, we are to:

- "...humble ourselves and pray..." Pride and self-sufficiency are snares of satan to get us to rely on our own strength, especially when we are trying to solve problems. That is the teaching of Secular Humanism.

- "...and seek my presence..." Solomon had sought God's wisdom and strength, acknowledging the people belonged to God and were Sovereignty. Jesus, when He prayed, acknowledged God's presence or prayed in thanksgiving for "...hearing My prayer."

- "...and turn from their evil ways..." this is perhaps the most misinterpreted part of this passage. God is not talking of specific sins, but evil defined as an attitude of purposely turning one's back on God's sovereignty in our lives. In the strategy we speak of here, each person who decides to take up this challenge of Spiritual Warrior must go to God and ask the Holy Spirit to reveal those areas of darkness in their life that prevents God's love from flowing through them. This is one of the strategies or prayers taught in 12 Step Spirituality — to have God remove deficiencies and defects of character to better serve Him.

In my mind, one concrete way we can "...turn from our evil ways..." is to let go of those issues that divide us as Christians, and focus on those things we do believe in: the Passion Story. We also can all agree upon the fact that God chose Mary from among all other women to be the Mother of Our Lord. I can almost hear God saying, "Stop that fighting! Am I going to have to turn this car around?"

God's Promise

The terms of the Covenant are that God will:

1. Hear us from Heaven. Psalm 50:14-15 tells us: *"Offer praise as your sacrifice to God; fulfill your vows to the Most High. Then call on me in time of distress; I will rescue you, and you shall honor me."* Read 2 Chronicles, Chapter 20 of how King Jehoshaphat followed these orders and the results that followed.

2. God pardons our sins. This is the complete victory of Our Lord Jesus Christ at the Cross and Resurrection. Our sins are pardoned and we are reconciled to God through the precious blood of His Son.

3. God will revive our land. It is not in the election of political officials or in the might of an army that our nation will be saved, but by the Grace and Mercy of our *loving God*!!

Think for a moment of 10—no 100, no 1,000, no 10,000—of God's children around the country using one single strategy to petition His intervention to deliver the United States from the evils that have come upon us. Imagine ten thousand or more people, becoming like little children asking our Father to fix the brokenness of this beautiful country.

I am the first to lay down my denominational pride and pick up the Rosary beads as my weapon.

How to Use This Book

While I used the Catholic Rosary as a guide through these prayers, you may or may not want to use a physical Rosary. For my non-Catholic brothers and sisters, you can purchase a Rosary through several resources. Either go to your local Christian bookstore, or you can order online.* I find much power in using the Rosary. Some people are "tactile" people and find great comfort in touching something as they pray. This will help them in that area. As I said before, the Rosary is a tool to keep focused on prayer. But I have also prayed the prayers in this book without a Rosary. Do what feels most comfortable to you. The important thing *is to pray for the healing of our country.*

The most power comes from daily prayer. Allow possibly 20 minutes to begin with each day to say the prayers in this book. It could take more time if you feel so moved. The decades of the Rosary may also be split into prayer times of shorter duration throughout the day.

Before you begin the prayers, find a quiet place, either a

quiet room in your house, or in your church, in your garden, at the lake… wherever you can focus and be free of daily distractions.

The next section explains how to pray the Rosary. The intercessions are prayers to begin your journey. You will then begin to pray for those who govern. Again, you can either use a physical Rosary or pray without a Rosary; God is more moved by your desire to heal America than He is in your performance. Your desire to please Him pleases Him.

Now, let us *pray without ceasing*…

* You may purchase a Rosary at our website: www.stuwalker.biz, at your local Catholic bookstore, or at the following online stores:

St. Patrick's Guild: http://www.stpatricksguild.com/

Holy Cross Books and Gifts: http://www.holycrossinc.com/storehours.html

The Prayers That Make Up the Rosary

The Rosary consists of a series of prayers, either those of beliefs Christians hold in common, or scripture passages that are prayed as petitions before God. Allow me to share what they symbolize.

The Sign of the Cross

Catholics have used the Sign of the Cross to acknowledge the prayers they are about to pray as holy and sanctified; set apart to worship God.

> *"In the name of the Father, the Son, and the Holy Spirit. Amen."*

The right hand is placed on the forehead (the symbol of our intellect and our will), lowered to the heart (symbol of life, surrendered to the Lord), and the left shoulder, then the right shoulder (symbol of the yoke Jesus asked us to take up and to learn from Him and with Him.) (Matthew 11:29)

Think about this for a moment. You have just called into your presence the Holy Trinity.

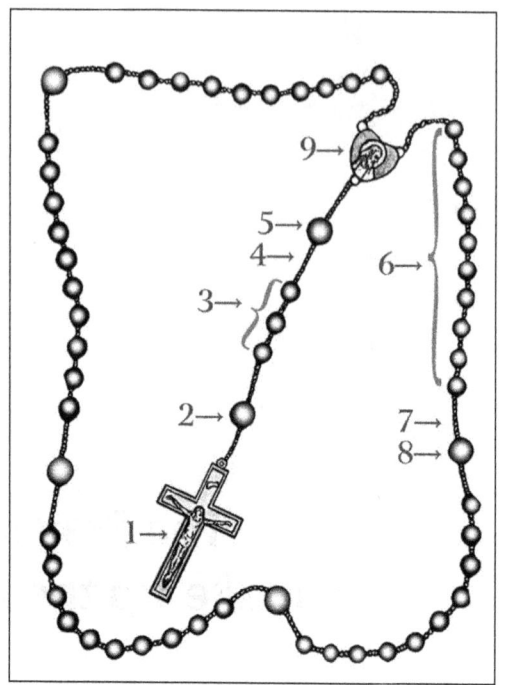

©Marian Fathers of the Immaculate Conception of the B.V.M.

The above diagram shows how to pray the Rosary. If you are new to this type of prayer, this diagram will help you on the journey. The number correlate to the numbers in the following text. Here's a quick guide to what the numbers relate to:

1. Make the sign of the cross and say the "Apostles' Creed."
2. Say the "Our Father."
3. Say three "Hail Marys."
4. Say the "Glory Be to the Father."
5. Announce the First Mystery; then say the "Our Father."
6. Say ten "Hail Marys," while meditating on the Mystery.
7. Say the "Glory Be to the Father." After each decade say the following prayer requested by the Blessed Virgin Mary at Fatima: "O my Jesus, forgive us our sins, save us from the fires of hell, lead all souls to Heaven, especially those in most need of Thy mercy."
8. Announce the Second Mystery; then say the "Our Father."

Repeat 6 and 7 and continue with the Third, Fourth, and Fifth Mysteries in the same manner.
9. Say the "Hail, Holy Queen" on the medal after the five decades are completed.

The Apostles' Creed

As you recite the Apostles' Creed, cradle the Cross gently in the palm of your hand. (Isaiah 49:16 tells us God holds us in the Palm of His hand, we return the affection in this prayer.) We reflect on the Passion of Christ; from the Last Supper to His Assumption and the descent of the Holy Spirit on Pentecost.

I believe in God, the Father almighty,
creator of heaven and earth.

I believe in Jesus Christ, His only Son, our Lord,
who was conceived by the Holy Spirit,
born of the Virgin Mary,
suffered under Pontius Pilate,
he descended to the dead.

On the third day he rose again;
he ascended into heaven,
he is seated at the right hand of the Father,
and he will come again to judge the living and the dead.

I believe in the Holy Spirit,
the holy catholic* church,
the communion of saints,
the forgiveness of sins,
the resurrection of the body,
and the life everlasting. *AMEN.*

(* The meaning here is universal. As mentioned earlier, when used with a capital "C," it refers to the denomination.)

For many, this is the universal statement of faith of all Christians. Here is a beautiful description of content:

This creed is called the Apostles' Creed not because it was produced by the apostles themselves but because it contains a brief summary of their teachings. It sets forth their doctrine "in sublime simplicity, in unsurpassable brevity, in beautiful order, and with liturgical solemnity." In its present form it is dated no later than the fourth century. More than any other Christian creed, it may justly be called an ecumenical symbol of faith.
—Christian Reformed Church (www.crcna.org/welcome/beliefs/creeds/apostles-creed)

We seek those truths we share as brothers and sisters in Christ, and this is one of those truths. Many denominations embrace the Apostles' Creed as a concise statement of faith.

The Our Father

This is a direct petition to God as taught by Jesus to His disciples about how to pray. The Our Fathers are listed as **#2, #5, and #8** on the Rosary diagram.

When you pray, do not be like the hypocrites, who love to stand and pray in the synagogues and on street corners so that others may see them. Amen, I say to you, they have received their reward. But when you pray, go to your inner room, close the door, and pray to your Father in secret. And your Father who sees in secret will repay you. In praying, do not babble like the pagans, who think that they will be heard because of their many words. Do not be like them. Your Father knows what you need before you ask him.

This is how you are to pray:

Our Father in heaven,

hallowed be your name,
your kingdom come, your will be done,
On earth as in heaven.
Give us today our daily bread;
and forgive us our debts,
as we forgive our debtors;
and do not subject us to the final test,
but deliver us from the evil one.
Matthew 6:5-14

This passage is found in the sixth chapter of Matthew, which means it is part of the Sermon on the Mount. The Sermon on the Mount encompasses the teachings of Jesus to those who were his "disciples," a word that denotes a new way of life.

The Hail Mary

The "Hail Mary" is a scripturally based prayer with a petition added at the end. It basically is the conversation between Mary and the angel Gabriel at the Annunciation. It is also part of the conversation between Mary and her cousin Elizabeth who also had a "miraculous" pregnancy, although not as supernatural as that of Mary. Catholics do not worship Mary as a Deity, rather, they *honor her* as chosen by God.

> Hail Mary,
> Full of Grace,
> The Lord is with Thee.
> Blessed are Thou among women,
> and blessed is the fruit of thy womb, Jesus.
>
> Holy Mary,
> Mother of God,
> Pray for us sinners,
> Now, and at the hour of our death. Amen.

Let's break that open:

> Hail, Mary, full of Grace, The Lord is with thee.
> **Luke 1:28**

> Blessed are you among women, and blessed is the fruit of your womb…
> **Luke 1:41-42**

For those who do not wish to pray, "Holy Mary, Mother of God," you are invited to pray, "**Holy Mary, *Mother of Jesus***, pray for us now and at the hour of our death. Amen."

The Glory Be

> "Glory be to the Father, to the Son, and to the Holy Spirit. Amen."

This, of course, is the Doxology prayed by many different denominations. While not the Catholic Doxology prayed by the Priest at Mass, it is the simple desire to give Glory to God rather than rely upon the strength of man.

The dictionary defines doxology as "an expression of praise to God, especially a short hymn sung as part of a Christian worship service." The word doxology comes from the Greek doxa, ("glory, splendor, grandeur") and logos, ("word" or "speaking"). Most doxologies are short hymns of praise to God in various Christian worship services, often added to the end of canticles, psalms, and hymns…

Although the word doxology is not found in the Bible, the themes expressed in doxologies are certainly scriptural. Praising God for His blessings (Ephesians 1:3), ascribing to Him all glory (Romans 11:36; Ephesians 3:21), and affirming the Trinity (Matthew 28:19) have always been integral parts of true Christian worship.

—www.gotquestions.org/doxology.html

The "Mysteries" of the Rosary

The "Mysteries" of the Rosary are meditations on various events in the Life of Jesus. They are for prayer and contemplation on the events of the life of Christ as lived out in His human condition. In our humanness, we like to celebrate certain events that impacted our lives and the lives of others. We will find that the mysteries are, in fact, based on events found in the four Gospels of Matthew, Mark, Luke, and John. Let's take a look.

The Five Joyful Mysteries

1. **The Annunciation**
   The angel Gabriel said, "Do not be afraid, Mary, you have found favor with God. You will conceive and bear a Son, and you shall call him Jesus." *Luke 1:30-31*

2. The Visitation
Mary visited her cousin, Elizabeth, who said to her, "Blessed are you among women and blessed is the fruit of your womb." *Luke 1:42*

3. The Birth of Jesus
Mary gave birth to her first-born son and wrapped him in swaddling clothes and laid him in a manger. *Luke 2:7*

4. The Presentation of Jesus in the Temple
When the time came...they brought the child up to Jerusalem to present him to the Lord. *Luke1:22*

5. The Finding of Jesus in the Temple
After three days they found Jesus in the Temple, sitting among the teachers and asking them questions. *Luke 1:46*

The Five Luminous Mysteries

These are called the "Mysteries of light," because they deal with the active ministries of Christ.

1. The Baptism of Jesus
Jesus came to Nazareth in the province of Galilee, and was baptized by John in the Jordan. *Mark 1:9*

2. The Wedding at Cana
There was a wedding in the town of Cana, in Galilee. Jesus' mother was there, and Jesus and his disciples had also been invited. *John 2:1*

3. The Proclamation of the Kingdom of God
Jesus went all over Galilee, teaching in the synagogues, preaching the Good News about the Kingdom, and healing people who had all kinds of diseases and sickness. *Mark 4:23*

4. The Transfiguration
Jesus took Peter, James, and John with him and went up a mountain to pray. While he was praying, his face changed, in appearance, and his clothes became dazzling white. *Luke 9:28-29*

5. The Institution of the Holy Eucharist
"I am the bread of life," Jesus told them, "Those who come to me will never be hungry; those who believe in me will never be thirsty." *John 6:35*

The Five Sorrowful Mysteries

1. The First Sorrowful Mystery:
The Agony in the Garden
They went to a place called Gethsemane...and Jesus became fearful and agitated. *Mark 14:32*

2. The Second Sorrowful Mystery:
The Scourging of Jesus at the Pillar
Pilate, wishing to please the crowd, released Barabbas, and had Jesus scourged. *Mark 15:15*

3. The Third Sorrowful Mystery:
Jesus is Crowned With Thorns
The soldiers clothed him in a purple cloak and placing a crown of thorns they put it on Him. *Mark 15:17*

4. The Fourth Sorrowful Mystery:
Jesus Carries His Cross
And he went out bearing His own cross, to the place of the skull, called Golgotha. *John 19:17*

5. **The Fifth Sorrowful Mystery:**
   The Crucifixion
   And they crucified Him, and divided His clothes among them casting lots to decide what each should take. *Mark 15:24*

The Five Glorious Mysteries

1. **The First Glorious Mystery:**
   The Resurrection
   The angel said, "Do not be afraid...He is not here, He is risen as He said." *Matthew 28:5-6*

2. **The Second Glorious Mystery:**
   The Ascension of Jesus
   As the apostles looked on, Jesus was taken up into heaven out of their sight. *Acts 1:9*

3. **The Third Glorious Mystery:**
   The Descent of the Holy Spirit
   They were filled with the Holy Spirit and began to speak in tongues as they were given power to speak. *Acts 2:2*

4. **The Fourth Glorious Mystery:**
   The Assumption of Mary Into Heaven*
   We believe that Jesus died and rose again. Through Jesus, God will bring to life those who have fallen asleep. *I Thessalonians 4:14*

5. **The Fifth Glorious Mystery:**
   The Coronation of the Blessed Virgin*
   A great sign appeared in the heavens, a woman clothed with the sun, the moon under her feet, and on her head a crown of twelve stars. *Rev 12:1*

*Again, it is not the goal of this booklet to convert anyone to Catholicism, but to establish the biblical foundation of the prayers. As we use "Spiritual" weapons for Spiritual warfare against enemies unseen, we stand in unity for the restoration to Judeo/Christian principles our nation was founded upon. United we stand.

Let the Intercession Begin

And now, we intentionally go into Spiritual Warfare for the United States of America using one of the most effective weapons of Spiritual Warfare that has been used for centuries to beg God's favor and mercy.

There are three battle cries that we use in our Spiritual Warfare to bring America back to Judeo/Christian principles.

The **first two** come from Our Lord Jesus Christ.

> If a kingdom is divided against itself, that kingdom cannot stand.
> And if a house is divided against itself, that house will not be able to stand.
> And if satan has risen up against himself and is divided, he cannot stand; that is the end of him.
> But no one can enter a strong man's house to plunder his property unless he first ties up the strong man. Then he can plunder his house.
>
> **Mark 3:24-27**

And when he (the Holy Spirit) comes he will convict the world in regard to sin and righteousness and condemnation: sin, because they do not believe in me; righteousness, because I am going to the Father and you will no longer see me; condemnation, because the ruler of this world has been condemned.

John 16:9-11

The third battle cry comes from man:

Soldiers! Let us humble ourselves before the Lord our God, asking through Christ the forgiveness of our sins, beseeching the aid of the God of our forefathers in the defense of our homes and our liberties, thanking Him for His past blessings and imploring their continuance upon our cause and our people.

Knowing that intercessory prayer is our mightiest weapon and the supreme call for all Christians today, I pleadingly urge our people everywhere to pray. Believing that prayer is the greatest contribution that our people can make to this critical hour, I humbly urge that we make time to pray - to really pray!

Let there be prayer at sunup, at noonday, at sundown, at midnight - all through the day. Let us pray for our children, our youth, our aged, our pastors, our homes. Let us pray for the churches.

Let us pray for ourselves, that we may not lose the word "concern" out of our Christian vocabulary. Let us pray for our nation. Let us pray for those who have never known Jesus Christ and His redeeming love, for moral forces

everywhere, for our national leaders. Let prayer be our passion. Let prayer be our practice.
General Robert E Lee, 1863

While this prayer may seem inappropriate because General Lee was on "the other side," it shows often we find our "enemies" are also praying for God's Will in their lives. The time we feel we have the "total truth" on any given subject, we find ourselves in error.

During the Civil War, one of President Lincoln's advisors told President Lincoln that he hoped God was on their side. Lincoln replied, in one of his more famous quotes, "Sir, my concern is not whether God is on our side; my greatest concern is to be on God's side, for God is always right."

As Christian soldiers, we are taught to pray, "Thy will be done..." The politics of General Lee or President Lincoln are not the point here, the petition it represents is a noble prayer for either side. In fact, General Lee's prayer was answered; God did bring unity to this country, just not the "unity" General Lee envisioned. How many times have we experienced that in our lives? We are responsible to turn to God in prayer and trust; God is responsible for the results.

Prayers for Those Who Govern

First of all, then, I ask that supplications, prayers, petitions, and thanksgivings be offered for everyone, for kings and for all in authority, that we may lead a quiet and tranquil life in all devotion and dignity. This is good and pleasing to God our savior, who wills everyone to be saved and to come to knowledge of the truth.
I Timothy 2:1-4

God Can Heal Our Nation and Bring Revival Through Prayer and Fasting

We are "...one nation, under God..." Whether people accept or reject God, they are still *His* creation. The fact that people do not believe or obey does not deny the existence of the God who loves them.

There are 50 Hail Mary's to be said in the Rosary and there are 50 States. If you choose to use a physical Rosary to pray these prayers, you will find numbers that relate to the Rosary diagram on page 26. Information on where you can purchase a Rosary is on page 24.

So, let us begin with a general opening prayer stating the goal of our prayers; that God will bring unity of purpose to the minds of all praying these Rosaries:

In the name of the Father, the Son, and the Holy Spirit. Amen.

For Unity of Purpose

Let us pray,

Mary, we start by acknowledging your specific place in the history of Mankind, as the one woman chosen by God to be the Mother of His Son, Our Lord, Jesus Christ. For your choice to say *yes* to the plan God had for your life, we thank you for your leadership as a role model for all of us to follow. One word, *yes*, to God's request, changed the life of all mankind for all eternity. Pray with us as we humble ourselves before God and pray:

The Apostles' Creed (1)

That God's Will Be Done...

Let us pray,
Our Father... (2)

For An Increase of Faith in All Christians

Let us pray,
Hail Mary... (3)

For an Increase in Hope Among All Christians

> Let us pray,
> Hail Mary... **(3)**

For an Increase in Love Among All Christians

> Let us pray,
> Hail Mary... **(3)**

That the Holy Spirit Will Give Us the Grace to Turn Back to God

> Let us pray...
> Glory be to the Father... **(4)**

Next you will pray the five decades. Remember, a decade is one Our Father and 10 Hail Mary's. Each day you will pray the five decades. When you are praying for a state (Hail Mary's), if the Holy Spirit brings to mind a circumstance, friend, or family member in that state, why not simply include that in your prayer at the end of the Hail Mary. The Mysteries are listed at the top of each decade and suggest days to focus on particular Mysteries.* The following is the suggested strategy for praying the Rosary during the week:

Monday and Saturday: The Joyful Mysteries on page 31
The first Decade of the Joyful Mysteries begins with the Annunciation

Tuesday and Friday: The Sorrowful Mysteries on page 33
The first Decade of the Sorrowful Mysteries begins with the Agony in the Garden

Wednesday and Sunday: The Glorious Mysteries on page 34
The first Decade of the Glorious Mysteries begins with the Resurrection

Thursday: The Luminous Mysteries on page 32
The first Decade of the Luminous Mysteries begins with The Baptism of Jesus

* The pattern here is followed with each set of Mysteries. For example, Monday, one would say the Joyful Mysteries. Tuesday, the Sorrowful Mysteries, and so on. There are simply seven days and four sets of mysteries. Where two sets of mysteries are listed for a given day (Tuesday and Friday: the first Sorrowful Mystery), it means that set of prayers are said on both days, separately. The pattern is repeated throughout the four sets of Mysteries.

The First Decade

For the Spiritual Leaders of All Faiths

Almighty God, in your love,
you bless your people with Spiritual leaders,
a sign of your faithfulness to your people. *1 Timothy 1:1-2*

We ask that you immerse them in the ocean of your Divine Mercy

Let us pray,

Recite the Mystery here (see pages 31-34 page 44) and then Our Father (5).

(6) *Hail Mary, full of Grace. The Lord is with thee and blessed art thou among women, and blessed is the fruit of thy womb — Jesus. Holy Mary, Mother of Our Lord, pray for the citizens of* **ALABAMA**, *now and at the hour of their death. Amen.*

Hail Mary, full of Grace. The Lord is with thee and blessed art thou among women, and blessed is the fruit of thy womb — Jesus. Holy Mary, Mother of Our Lord, pray for the citizens of **ALASKA**, *now and at the hour of their death. Amen.*

Hail Mary, full of Grace. The Lord is with thee and blessed art thou among women, and blessed is the fruit of thy womb — Jesus. Holy Mary, Mother of Our Lord, pray for the citizens of **ARIZONA**, *now and at the hour of their death. Amen.*

Hail Mary, full of Grace. The Lord is with thee and blessed art thou among women, and blessed is the fruit of thy womb —

Jesus. Holy Mary, Mother of Our Lord, pray for the citizens of **ARKANSAS**, now and at the hour of their death. Amen.

Hail Mary, full of Grace. The Lord is with thee and blessed art thou among women, and blessed is the fruit of thy womb — Jesus. Holy Mary, Mother of Our Lord, pray for the citizens of **CALIFORNIA**, now and at the hour of their death. Amen.

Hail Mary, full of Grace. The Lord is with thee and blessed art thou among women, and blessed is the fruit of thy womb — Jesus. Holy Mary, Mother of Our Lord, pray for the citizens of **COLORADO**, now and at the hour of their death. Amen.

Hail Mary, full of Grace. The Lord is with thee and blessed art thou among women, and blessed is the fruit of thy womb — Jesus. Holy Mary, Mother of Our Lord, pray for the citizens of **CONNECTICUT**, now and at the hour of their death. Amen.

Hail Mary, full of Grace. The Lord is with thee and blessed art thou among women, and blessed is the fruit of thy womb — Jesus. Holy Mary, Mother of Our Lord, pray for the citizens of **DELAWARE**, now and at the hour of their death. Amen.

Hail Mary, full of Grace. The Lord is with thee and blessed art thou among women, and blessed is the fruit of thy womb — Jesus. Holy Mary, Mother of Our Lord, pray for the citizens of **FLORIDA**, now and at the hour of their death. Amen.

Hail Mary, full of Grace. The Lord is with thee and blessed art thou among women, and blessed is the fruit of thy womb — Jesus. Holy Mary, Mother of Our Lord, pray for the citizens of **GEORGIA**, now and at the hour of their death. Amen.

PETITION: That the Holy Spirit Grants Us the Grace to Turn Back to God

Let us pray...
Glory be to the Father...(7)

Oh my Jesus, forgive us our sins, save us from the fires of hell; lead all souls to heaven, especially those in most need of thy mercy.

The Second Decade

[Follow the same pattern as listed for the First Decade.]

GOD THE FATHER

The Executive Branch

The President of the United States; for the Governors of each state; and for all municipal and local leaders

We ask that you immerse them in the ocean of your Divine Mercy

Let us pray,

Recite the Mystery here (see pages 31-34 page 44) and then Our Father (8).

Hail Mary, full of Grace. The Lord is with thee and blessed art thou among women, and blessed is the fruit of thy womb — Jesus. Holy Mary, Mother of Our Lord, pray for the citizens of **HAWAII**, *now and at the hour of their death. Amen.*

Hail Mary, full of Grace. The Lord is with thee and blessed art thou among women, and blessed is the fruit of thy womb — Jesus. Holy Mary, Mother of Our Lord, pray for the citizens of **IDAHO**, *now and at the hour of their death. Amen.*

Hail Mary, full of Grace. The Lord is with thee and blessed art thou among women, and blessed is the fruit of thy womb — Jesus. Holy Mary, Mother of Our Lord, pray for the citizens of **ILLINOIS**, *now and at the hour of their death. Amen.*

Hail Mary, full of Grace. The Lord is with thee and blessed

art thou among women, and blessed is the fruit of thy womb —
Jesus. Holy Mary, Mother of Our Lord, pray for the citizens of
INDIANA, now and at the hour of their death. Amen.

Hail Mary, full of Grace. The Lord is with thee and blessed
art thou among women, and blessed is the fruit of thy womb —
Jesus. Holy Mary, Mother of Our Lord, pray for the citizens of
IOWA, now and at the hour of their death. Amen.

Hail Mary, full of Grace. The Lord is with thee and blessed
art thou among women, and blessed is the fruit of thy womb —
Jesus. Holy Mary, Mother of Our Lord, pray for the citizens of
KANSAS, now and at the hour of their death. Amen.

Hail Mary, full of Grace. The Lord is with thee and blessed
art thou among women, and blessed is the fruit of thy womb —
Jesus. Holy Mary, Mother of Our Lord, pray for the citizens of
KENTUCKY, now and at the hour of their death. Amen.

Hail Mary, full of Grace. The Lord is with thee and blessed
art thou among women, and blessed is the fruit of thy womb —
Jesus. Holy Mary, Mother of Our Lord, pray for the citizens of
LOUISIANA, now and at the hour of their death. Amen.

Hail Mary, full of Grace. The Lord is with thee and blessed
art thou among women, and blessed is the fruit of thy womb —
Jesus. Holy Mary, Mother of Our Lord, pray for the citizens of
MAINE, now and at the hour of their death. Amen.

Hail Mary, full of Grace. The Lord is with thee and blessed
art thou among women, and blessed is the fruit of thy womb —
Jesus. Holy Mary, Mother of Our Lord, pray for the citizens of
MARYLAND, now and at the hour of their death. Amen.

PETITION: That the Holy Spirit Grants Us the Grace to Turn Back to God

Let us pray...
Glory be to the Father...

Oh my Jesus, forgive us our sins, save us from the fires of hell; lead all souls to heaven, especially those in most need of thy mercy.

The Third Decade

GOD THE SON

The Legistlative Branches
For the Senate and Congress at both Federal and State levels

We ask that you immerse them in the ocean of your Divine Mercy

---

Any law that is passed that does not have as its foundation moral law, is not a just law.
—Martin Luther King, Jr.

Let us pray,

Recite the Mystery here (see pages 31-34 page 44) and then Our Father.

Hail Mary, full of Grace. The Lord is with thee and blessed art thou among women, and blessed is the fruit of thy womb — Jesus. Holy Mary, Mother of Our Lord, pray for the citizens of **MASSACHUSETTS**, now and at the hour of their death. Amen.

Hail Mary, full of Grace. The Lord is with thee and blessed art thou among women, and blessed is the fruit of thy womb — Jesus. Holy Mary, Mother of Our Lord, pray for the citizens of **MICHIGAN**, now and at the hour of their death. Amen.

Hail Mary, full of Grace. The Lord is with thee and blessed art thou among women, and blessed is the fruit of thy womb — Jesus. Holy Mary, Mother of Our Lord, pray for the citizens of **MINNESOTA**, now and at the hour of their death. Amen.

Hail Mary, full of Grace. The Lord is with thee and blessed art thou among women, and blessed is the fruit of thy womb — Jesus. Holy Mary, Mother of Our Lord, pray for the citizens of **MISSISSIPPI**, now and at the hour of their death. Amen.

Hail Mary, full of Grace. The Lord is with thee and blessed art thou among women, and blessed is the fruit of thy womb — Jesus. Holy Mary, Mother of Our Lord, pray for the citizens of **MISSOURI**, now and at the hour of their death. Amen.

Hail Mary, full of Grace. The Lord is with thee and blessed art thou among women, and blessed is the fruit of thy womb — Jesus. Holy Mary, Mother of Our Lord, pray for the citizens of **MONTANA**, now and at the hour of their death. Amen.

Hail Mary, full of Grace. The Lord is with thee and blessed art thou among women, and blessed is the fruit of thy womb — Jesus. Holy Mary, Mother of Our Lord, pray for the citizens of **NEBRASKA**, now and at the hour of their death. Amen.

Hail Mary, full of Grace. The Lord is with thee and blessed art thou among women, and blessed is the fruit of thy womb — Jesus. Holy Mary, Mother of Our Lord, pray for the citizens of **NEVADA**, now and at the hour of their death. Amen.

Hail Mary, full of Grace. The Lord is with thee and blessed art thou among women, and blessed is the fruit of thy womb — Jesus. Holy Mary, Mother of Our Lord, pray for the citizens of **NEW HAMPSHIRE**, now and at the hour of their death. Amen.

Hail Mary, full of Grace. The Lord is with thee and blessed art thou among women, and blessed is the fruit of thy womb — Jesus. Holy Mary, Mother of Our Lord, pray for the citizens of **NEW JERSEY**, *now and at the hour of their death. Amen.*

PETITION: That the Holy Spirit Grants Us the Grace to Turn Back to God

Let us pray...
Glory be to the Father...

Oh my Jesus, forgive us our sins, save us from the fires of hell; lead all souls to heaven, especially those in most need of thy mercy.

The Fourth Decade

GOD THE HOLY SPIRIT

The Judiciary Branches

For the US Supreme Court; for the State and Supreme Courts; for all Federal and State Court Systems

We ask that you immerse them in the ocean of your Divine Mercy

Let us pray,

Recite the Mystery here (see pages 31-34 page 44) and then Our Father.

Hail Mary, full of Grace. The Lord is with thee and blessed art thou among women, and blessed is the fruit of thy womb — Jesus. Holy Mary, Mother of Our Lord, pray for the citizens of **NEW MEXICO**, *now and at the hour of their death. Amen.*

Hail Mary, full of Grace. The Lord is with thee and blessed art thou among women, and blessed is the fruit of thy womb — Jesus. Holy Mary, Mother of Our Lord, pray for the citizens of **NEW YORK**, *now and at the hour of their death. Amen.*

Hail Mary, full of Grace. The Lord is with thee and blessed art thou among women, and blessed is the fruit of thy womb — Jesus. Holy Mary, Mother of Our Lord, pray for the citizens of **NORTH CAROLINA**, *now and at the hour of their death. Amen.*

Hail Mary, full of Grace. The Lord is with thee and blessed art thou among women, and blessed is the fruit of thy womb — Jesus. Holy Mary, Mother of Our Lord, pray for the citizens of **NORTH DAKOTA**, now and at the hour of their death. Amen.

Hail Mary, full of Grace. The Lord is with thee and blessed art thou among women, and blessed is the fruit of thy womb — Jesus. Holy Mary, Mother of Our Lord, pray for the citizens of **OHIO**, now and at the hour of their death. Amen.

Hail Mary, full of Grace. The Lord is with thee and blessed art thou among women, and blessed is the fruit of thy womb — Jesus. Holy Mary, Mother of Our Lord, pray for the citizens of **OKLAHOMA**, now and at the hour of their death. Amen.

Hail Mary, full of Grace. The Lord is with thee and blessed art thou among women, and blessed is the fruit of thy womb — Jesus. Holy Mary, Mother of Our Lord, pray for the citizens of **OREGON**, now and at the hour of their death. Amen.

Hail Mary, full of Grace. The Lord is with thee and blessed art thou among women, and blessed is the fruit of thy womb — Jesus. Holy Mary, Mother of Our Lord, pray for the citizens of **PENNSYLVANIA**, now and at the hour of their death. Amen.

Hail Mary, full of Grace. The Lord is with thee and blessed art thou among women, and blessed is the fruit of thy womb — Jesus. Holy Mary, Mother of Our Lord, pray for the citizens of **RHODE ISLAND**, now and at the hour of their death. Amen.

Hail Mary, full of Grace. The Lord is with thee and blessed art thou among women, and blessed is the fruit of thy womb — Jesus. Holy Mary, Mother of Our Lord, pray for the citizens of **SOUTH CAROLINA**, now and at the hour of their death. Amen.

PETITION: That the Holy Spirit Grants Us the Grace to Turn Back to God

Let us pray...
Glory be to the Father...

Oh my Jesus, forgive us our sins, save us from the fires of hell; lead all souls to heaven, especially those in most need of thy mercy.

The Fifth Decade

For the Warriors Who Protect Us
For those who serve in the military, police, fire, and EMS, who willingly place themselves in harms way for our safety and protection

We ask that you immerse them in the ocean of your Divine Mercy

Let us pray,

Recite the Mystery here (see pages 31-34 page 44) and then Our Father.

Hail Mary, full of Grace. The Lord is with thee and blessed art thou among women, and blessed is the fruit of thy womb — Jesus. Holy Mary, Mother of Our Lord, pray for the citizens of **SOUTH DAKOTA**, now and at the hour of their death. Amen.

Hail Mary, full of Grace. The Lord is with thee and blessed art thou among women, and blessed is the fruit of thy womb — Jesus. Holy Mary, Mother of Our Lord, pray for the citizens of **TENNESSEE**, now and at the hour of their death. Amen.

Hail Mary, full of Grace. The Lord is with thee and blessed art thou among women, and blessed is the fruit of thy womb — Jesus. Holy Mary, Mother of Our Lord, pray for the citizens of **TEXAS**, now and at the hour of their death. Amen.

Hail Mary, full of Grace. The Lord is with thee and blessed art thou among women, and blessed is the fruit of thy womb —

Jesus. Holy Mary, Mother of Our Lord, pray for the citizens of **UTAH**, now and at the hour of their death. Amen.

Hail Mary, full of Grace. The Lord is with thee and blessed art thou among women, and blessed is the fruit of thy womb — Jesus. Holy Mary, Mother of Our Lord, pray for the citizens of **VERMONT**, now and at the hour of their death. Amen.

Hail Mary, full of Grace. The Lord is with thee and blessed art thou among women, and blessed is the fruit of thy womb — Jesus. Holy Mary, Mother of Our Lord, pray for the citizens of **VIRGINIA**, now and at the hour of their death. Amen.

Hail Mary, full of Grace. The Lord is with thee and blessed art thou among women, and blessed is the fruit of thy womb — Jesus. Holy Mary, Mother of Our Lord, pray for the citizens of **WASHINGTON**, now and at the hour of their death. Amen.

Hail Mary, full of Grace. The Lord is with thee and blessed art thou among women, and blessed is the fruit of thy womb — Jesus. Holy Mary, Mother of Our Lord, pray for the citizens of **WEST VIRGINIA**, now and at the hour of their death. Amen.

Hail Mary, full of Grace. The Lord is with thee and blessed art thou among women, and blessed is the fruit of thy womb — Jesus. Holy Mary, Mother of Our Lord, pray for the citizens of **WISCONSIN**, now and at the hour of their death. Amen.

Hail Mary, full of Grace. The Lord is with thee and blessed art thou among women, and blessed is the fruit of thy womb — Jesus. Holy Mary, Mother of Our Lord, pray for the citizens of **WYOMING**, now and at the hour of their death. Amen.

PETITION: That the Holy Spirit Grants Us the Grace to Turn Back to God

Let us pray...
Glory be to the Father...

Oh my Jesus, forgive us our sins, save us from the fires of hell; lead all souls to heaven, especially those in most need of thy mercy.

Hail, Holy Queen (9)

Hail, holy Queen, Mother of mercy, our life, our sweetness and our hope.
To thee do we cry, poor banished children of Eve:
to thee do we send up our sighs, mourning and weeping in this vale of tears.
Turn then, most gracious Advocate, thine eyes of mercy toward us,
and after this our exile, show unto us the blessed fruit of thy womb, Jesus.
O merciful, O loving, O sweet Virgin Mary! Amen.

As we finish our prayers of Spiritual Warfare, let us recall the words Mary spoke in response to Elizabeth's greeting:

And Mary said:

My soul proclaims the greatness of the Lord;
my spirit rejoices in God my savior.
For he has looked upon his handmaid's lowliness;

behold, from now on will all ages call me blessed.
The Mighty One has done great things for me,
and holy is his name.

His mercy is from age to age to those who fear him.
He has shown might with his arm,
dispersed the arrogant of mind and heart.
He has thrown down the rulers from their thrones but lifted up the lowly.
The hungry he has filled with good things; the rich he has sent away empty.
He has helped Israel his servant, remembering his mercy,
according to his promise to our fathers, to Abraham and to his descendants forever. *Luke 1:46-55*

The focus is not on Mary, but upon her *servant's heart*, an example for all of us. Like Mary, we acknowledge that it is God who is our Savior, and it is He who will call the United States back into order.

All generations have called her blessed — chosen by God for His instrument in Salvation — as he calls you and me in our day and age. As she reminds us, "His mercy is from age to age for those who fear (reverence) Him."

As mentioned earlier in this book, at the Wedding of Cana, Mary petitioned Jesus, "They are out of wine." Her desire was that the wedding party should not be embarrassed, but be "saved." She did not "instruct" Jesus on what to do, however, she did instruct the stewards, "Do as He tells you to do." You and I are told to pray unceasingly and pray for our enemies. Our enemies are those who would harm the United States of America, whether that harm come from outside our borders, or within our borders. Any person or group that encourages us to turn our back on God is our enemy. Jesus taught us to pray,

"...lead us not into temptation, but deliver us from evil."

Let us thank God for this opportunity to thank and praise him for choosing Mary. We remember that it is her consent to obey the will of God that led to the "fruit of your womb!"

> For a child is born to us,
> a son is given us;
> upon his shoulder dominion rests.
> They name him Wonder-Counselor,
> God-Hero,
> Father-Forever,
> Prince of Peace.
>
> **Isaiah 9:5**

Because this young woman, as a teenager, said "YES" to God, Eternity was changed forever. You and I can now be reconciled to God, who created us to be with Him. All the great leaders of the Kingdom of God, starting with Abraham, Moses, Mary, and others have always had an Intercessory Heart as part of their Gratitude to God for His Love.

Thank you for joining us in prayerful unity among Christian brothers and sisters who believe that God answers prayers. You may not be able to pray the Rosary each day. The more often you pray, the more often people around the nation will be strngthened and God will see His people are serious about repentence. He will heal our land, as is God's promise in 2nd Chronicles 7:14 (page 20). It is never in God's Will to bring disaster or calamity to His people or to a nation. However, when the people tell Him to leave, He will. The consequences of that choice will be for the people to deal with. In reading the newspaper and watching TV news, that does not seem to be working very well, here or around the world.

The one principle of God's love is His forgiveness. He desires His children to return to Him so He can heal and once again prosper us as a Nation. Any parent knov·s that when a child becomes defiant, that child needs to be chastised and the intent of that parent is always to bring the child back into relationship with the family.

Remember always that God loves you, and as we pray together: GOD BLESS AMERICA!!

To order additional copies or to subscribe to our newsletter, visit our website:

www.stuwalker.biz

There is a discount at our website when you buy two print copies (one to give to a Protestant friend), and other offers. Also, you can subscribe to our newsletter which is sent weekly to aid in your Spiritual Growth.

www.ingramcontent.com/pod-product-compliance
Lightning Source LLC
Chambersburg PA
CBHW071313060426
42444CB00034B/2163